MW01593337

THE
Extraordinary
LIFE

DR. ERNEST CHILDS, TH.D.

To order more copies of *The Extraordinary Life*, contact
Dr. Ernest Childs:

Dr. Ernest Childs
Cross Communications
101 Mario Drive
Shelby, NC 28150

All Scripture quotations are from the King James Version
of the Bible.

The Extraordinary Life

Cover design: Mack Swaringen
Cover photo: http://www.istockphoto.com
Cover photo title: "Evening colored view of Everest from
Kala Patthar."
Design and page layout: Andrew Minion

Printed in Canada.

ISBN 978-0-9712414-8-0

Dedication

To my adopted son and his wife,
Evangelist Billy and Christy Ingram.
Their constant encouragement and
care for me can never be repaid.

Table of Contents

Preface

If the Epistle to the Romans is, as some have called it "The Himalayas of the Bible," then the section of chapters 5–8 is Mount Everest. Here we have the great doctrines of Justification by faith, Sanctification, Identification, and the Revelation of God's plan for successful living.

For many years after my conversion, I struggled with the knowledge that I ought to be a better Christian, live a more godly life, and have regular victory over sin, but I never really began to achieve that until the Holy Spirit very graciously opened my heart and understanding to the great truths set forth in these mountain peaks of Scripture. That is not to say that I have attained to all the truth in these chapters, but what God has shown me has resulted, over these last years, in a dramatic change in my life and ministry.

What I wish to share in these pages is some of the great truths God has shown me, with the prayer that these truths will be beneficial to all who read these pages.

I must acknowledge at the outset that the truths of which I write are not original with me. I stand on the shoulders of many great men of the past whose writings and preaching have influenced me greatly. As I write these words, my prayer is that the Holy Spirit will enlighten many to the

Biblical truths I have attempted to set forth. I can pray no other prayer than that of the Apostle Paul in Ephesians 1:17–19: *"That the God of our Lord Jesus Christ, the Father of glory, may give unto you the spirit of wisdom and revelation in the knowledge of him: the eyes of your understanding being enlightened; that ye may know what is the hope of his calling, and what the riches of the glory of his inheritance in the saints, and what is the exceeding greatness of his power to usward who believe...."*

May God bless you!

Acknowledgements

I make few claims to originality for this book and wish to acknowledge my heartfelt appreciation and indebtedness to those men and some women whose preaching and writings have been used of God to teach me the wonderful, life-changing Biblical truths of the victorious Christian life.

This book is the outgrowth of a series of messages and adult Sunday school lessons presented in two churches pastored over a period of twenty years.

I wish to acknowledge Miss Kelly Guisinger's many hours of labor in typing, proof-reading, and multitude of other tasks needed to bring this book into being.

Chapter 1
The Results of Justification by Faith

Therefore being justified by faith, we have peace with God through our Lord Jesus Christ: By whom also we have access by faith into this grace wherein we stand, and rejoice in hope of the glory of God. And not only so, but we glory in tribulations also: knowing that tribulation worketh patience: And patience, experience; and experience, hope: And hope maketh not ashamed; because the love of God is shed abroad in our hearts by the Holy Ghost which is given unto us. For when we were yet without strength, in due time Christ died for the ungodly. For scarcely for a righteous man will one die: yet peradventure for a good man some would even dare to die. But God commendeth his love toward us, in that, while we were yet sinners, Christ died for us. Much more then, being now justified by his blood, we shall be saved from wrath through him. For if, when we were enemies, we were reconciled to God by the death of his Son, much more, being reconciled, we shall be saved by his life. And not only so, but we also joy in God through our Lord Jesus Christ, by whom we have now received the atonement. Romans 5:1–11

Successful living from God's point of view begins with what theologians call Justification, which simply means being declared righteous by God through faith in the finished work of Christ. The verses above set forth nine results of being justified by faith. They are as follows:

v. 1: Peace with God
v. 2: Access to God
v. 2: Standing with God
v. 2: Hope in glory
v. 3: Triumph in trials
v. 5: God's love in our hearts
v. 5: The Holy Spirit
v. 9: Saved from wrath
v. 11: Joy in God

Let us now look at these individually.

Peace with God. Chapters 3 and 4 set forth Justification by faith by definition (3:21–31) and by illustration (chapter 4). Then, 5:1 begins with *"therefore,"* or in other words, "as a result of already having been declared righteous." It is not a process of being justified, but it is something that took place in the past with everlasting results. You cannot be more justified. It happened suddenly, totally, and forever when you believed. When you received Christ, you were declared righteous **forever** by God. You can never be more righteous and you will never be less righteous as far as God is concerned. As a result of "having been justified" by faith, I have peace with God, not just peace, but peace *with God*. This involves three truths.

1. God has fully judged our sins in Christ, our Substitute.

Surely he hath borne our griefs, and carried our sorrows: yet we did esteem him stricken, smitten of God, and afflicted. But he was wounded for our transgressions, he was bruised for our iniquities: the chastisement of our peace was upon him; and with his stripes we are healed. All we like sheep have gone astray; we have turned every one to his own way; and the LORD hath laid on him the iniquity of us all. Is. 53:4–6

2. God was so wholly satisfied with Christ's sacrifice that He will **never** bring up our sin again. (Heb. 10:17–18; Is. 44:22)

3. God is, therefore, at rest about us forever, no matter how weak, how stumbling our walk, how poor our understanding.

God looks at Christ's blood, not at our sins and weaknesses. All claims against us were settled when Christ *"...made peace through the blood of his cross..."* (Col. 1:20).

This peace **with** God is not a result of what He is now doing but what He has already done and is not to be confused with the "peace **of** God" (Phil. 4:7). Peace **with** God refers to our standing which is unchangeable, while the peace **of** God refers to our state which fluctuates with circumstances. One may have peace with God without having the peace of God, but it is impossible to have the peace of God without having peace with God.

Charles Price defines peace with God as follows: "That tranquil state of mind and emotions which results from the assurance that sins are forgiven and the believer no longer faces condemnation for sin."

This is only available in and through the finished work of Christ at Calvary.

Peace I leave with you, my peace I give unto you: not as the world giveth, give I unto you. Let not your heart be troubled, neither let it be afraid. Jn. 14:27

But he was wounded for our transgressions, he was bruised for our iniquities: the chastisement of our peace was upon him; and with his stripes we are healed. Is. 53:5

For he is our peace, who hath made both one, and hath broken down the middle wall of partition between us. Eph. 2:14

As a result of being justified by faith, we have peace with God.

> I hear the words of love,
> I gaze upon the blood,
> I see the mighty sacrifice,
> I have peace with God.
>
> 'Tis everlasting peace
> Sure as Jehovah's Name;
> 'Tis stable as His steadfast throne
> Forevermore the same.

Access to God. The word "access" means approach. Because we are justified by faith, we can approach God. He is not inaccessible to any believer. However, the unbeliever has no right to approach God for anything but salvation. When we have trusted Christ as Savior, then we have access through Him by the Holy Spirit.

For through him we both have access by one Spirit unto the Father. Eph. 2:18

In whom we have boldness and access with confidence by the faith of him. Eph. 3:12

This marvelous benefit has only been available since the crucifixion. In the Old Testament tabernacle and temple worship, only one person had access to God.

Now when these things were thus ordained, the priests went always into the first tabernacle, accomplishing the service of God. But into the second went the high priest alone once every year, not without blood, which he offered for himself, and for the errors of the people. Heb. 9:6–8, 11

In Matthew 27:50–51, we are told that when Jesus, "… *yielded up the ghost…the veil of the temple was rent in twain (two) from the top to the bottom….*" This veil separated the holy place from the Holy of Holies where only the high priest could enter once a year. The veil being rent signifies open access to God by any believer.

If you are a child of God, you have freedom to enter the presence of God at any time through the favor of Another, even Jesus Christ.

Standing with God. How can a sinner stand in the presence of a holy God?

Therefore the ungodly shall not stand in the judgment nor sinners in the congregation of the righteous. Psalm 1:5

If thou, LORD, shouldest mark iniquities, O Lord, who shall stand? Ps. 130:3

In Revelation 6:17, the wicked cry out "…*who shall be able to stand?*" If God were to pick out the iniquities in our lives, we could not stand that scouting. Before we were saved, we were outside of God with no standing whatsoever

(Eph. 2:12–13), but having been declared righteous by faith, our standing before God can be seen in three different ways:

Sons of God, John 1:12; Gal. 3:26

Kings and Priests, Rev. 1:5–6

Heirs of God, Rom. 8:14–17

It is important to recognize that that is maintained in the same way it was acquired—by faith through grace, not by our works or our character. It is all of grace.

The Hope of Glory. This is the future of the believer. We have a hope of the glory of God.

For the grace of God that bringeth salvation hath appeared to all men, teaching us that, denying ungodliness and worldly lusts, we should live soberly, righteously, and godly in this present world; looking for that blessed hope, and the glorious appearing of the great God and our Saviour, Jesus Christ. (Titus 2:11–13) While the "blessed hope" here has reference to the Rapture of the church, when Christ returns in the clouds to catch away His bride, the hope of the glory of God is also a blessed hope.

What is the "glory of God"? It is simply the likeness of God. God's glory is what God **is** in character, and Jesus Christ is the express image of the Father. (Heb. 1:3: *Who being the brightness of his glory, and the express image of his person, and upholding all things by the word of his power, when he had by himself purged our sins, sat down on the right hand of the Majesty on high;*). Our hope is to be like Him. (Rom.

8:29: *For whom he did foreknow, he also did predestinate to be conformed to the image of his Son, that he might be the firstborn among many brethren.*) God is working on that day-by-day in each of us; however, it will not be completed here, but rather at the rapture.

Beloved, now are we the sons of God, and it doth not yet appear what we shall be: but we know that, when he shall appear, we shall be like him; for we shall see him as he is. I Jn. 3:2

To whom God would make known what is the riches of the glory of this mystery among the Gentiles; which is Christ in you, the hope of glory. Col. 1:27

Triumph in Trials. Not only do we have hope of the glory of God, but we also glory in tribulations (v. 3). Everyone has trials, but the unsaved do not understand the purpose for trials and, thus, do not glory in them. Justification by faith does not mean there will be no trials or pressure, but when those trials come, we can glory in the purpose for them. James 1:2–3: *My brethren, count it all joy when ye fall into divers temptations; Knowing this, that the trying of your faith worketh patience.* If we have trusted Christ as Savior, one of the results should be rejoicing in the face of all kinds of trials.

The Thessalonians were suffering great trials because of their faith, so much so that they thought they were in the Great Tribulation. In II Thess. 1:4, Paul wrote, *"So that we ourselves glory in you in the churches of God for your patience and faith in all your persecutions that ye endure."* Paul could write this because of his own attitude in suffering in II Corinthians 4:8–9: *"…troubled, but not distressed; perplexed, but not in despair; persecuted, but not forsaken; cast down, but not destroyed"* because he recognized the purpose of his trials (v. 17).

We are exhorted in Romans 12:12 to *"...be patient in tribulation."* Someone has well-said, "If you do not want tribulation, do not ask the Lord for patience." The only way that patience can be developed is through tribulation. A pastor who changes churches every time a problem arises will never be able to deal with any of the pressures of life. A Christian who changes jobs, residences, or churches every time a problem arises will always be running.

How does the world deal with pressure? A bottle or pills or some other type of mechanism. How should you deal with pressure? Rejoice! Tribulation perfects patience, which perfects experience, which perfects hope, "and hope maketh not ashamed."

The Love of God. Every Christian has accepted the love of God for them as shown on Calvary. However, with all too many of us, that love comes in, but none goes out. The word "love" here is *agape*, the same as in verse 8 and in John 3:16. This love is not a selfish love, but rather a giving love. It is the love of God that loves the ungodly and undeserving. God's love is shed abroad in our hearts. The original language has the idea of being poured out or running greedily out. Our hearts should be so overflowing with the love of God that it is seen in our attitude, our speech, our actions, our thoughts, and our deeds. If you love only those that love you or do for you, then the outflow of God's love has been blocked, and you will become bitter and useless for God.

The Holy Ghost. John 7:38–39: *He that believeth on me, as the scripture hath said, out of his belly shall flow rivers of living water. 39 (But this spake he of the Spirit, which they that believe on him should receive: for the Holy Ghost was not yet given; because that Jesus was not yet glorified.)* John 14:16, 26: *And I will pray the Father, and he shall give you another Comforter, that he may abide with you for ever; 26 But the Comforter, which is the Holy Ghost, whom the Father will send in my name, he shall teach you all things, and bring all things to your remembrance, whatsoever I have said unto you.*

On the day of Pentecost, the Holy Spirit came to indwell every believer. At the moment you trusted Jesus Christ as your Savior, the Holy Spirit baptized you into Christ—*For by one Spirit are we all baptized into one body, whether we be Jews or Gentiles, whether we be bond or free; and have been all made to drink into one Spirit* (I Cor. 12:13)—and at the same time, came into your body—*What? know ye not that your body is the temple of the Holy Ghost which is in you, which ye have of God, and ye are not your own?* (I Cor. 6:19).

How do you know you have the Holy Spirit dwelling within you? Nowhere in Scripture does it ever say or imply that a result of the indwelling Spirit is speaking in tongues, prophesying, healing, or any other "sign."

Here the Scripture says it is a result of justification by faith. You know you have the Holy Spirit within, not because of some outward sign, but because you have trusted Jesus as

Savior. Please note in John 14:16 written above, that He has come to live within *forever*.

The last two benefits of being justified by faith are given in verses 9–11.

Saved from Wrath. This has a temporal and eternal application. The eternal application has to do with being saved from eternal condemnation and suffering in the Lake of Fire. (John 3:26; Rom. 1:18) According to John 3:18, the unbeliever is condemned already—*He that believeth on him is not condemned: but he that believeth not is condemned already, because he hath not believed in the name of the only begotten Son of God*—and that condemnation is the Lake of Fire. Rev. 20:15: *And whosoever was not found written in the book of life was cast into the lake of fire.* However, having been declared righteous on the grounds of Christ's shed blood, the wrath of God for sin under which all mankind stands condemned, was borne by Jesus Christ on Calvary. Everyone who flees to Him and accepts His payment is saved from wrath.

There is therefore now no condemnation to them which are in Christ Jesus… Rom. 8:1. We shall not have a part in the Lake of Fire because we are already delivered from it by Jesus. Not only are we delivered from the eternal wrath of God in the Lake of Fire, but we are also delivered from the temporal wrath of God in the Tribulation after the Rapture of the Church. This Great Tribulation is described in Revelation chapters 6–19. In those chapters, "the wrath of God" is used thirteen times.

And said to the mountains and rocks, Fall on us, and hide us from the face of him that sitteth on the throne, and from the wrath of the Lamb: For the great day of his wrath is come; and who shall be able to stand? Rev. 6:16–17

All the horrors of the Great Tribulation are poured out on mankind during a seven-year period, but we shall be delivered from that.

And to wait for his Son from heaven, whom he raised from the dead, even Jesus, which delivered us from the wrath to come. I Thes. 1:10

Because thou hast kept the word of my patience, I also will keep thee from the hour of temptation, which shall come upon all the world, to try them that dwell upon the earth. Rev. 3:10

We are saved from the eternal wrath of God and the temporal wrath of God through Jesus' finished work on our behalf.

The last benefit of Justification is ***Joy in God*** (verse 11). The word means to exult or glory in God. What a difference Justification makes! Chapter 3, verse 19 says, "*…that every mouth may be stopped and all the world may become guilty before God.*" But 5:1 says, "*…being justified by faith…through our Lord Jesus Christ…*" Now, we exult, we glory, we rejoice through our Lord Jesus Christ because by Him, we have received reconciliation. That is, we have been reconciled or brought back to God.

This benefit takes us back to 3:27: "*Where is boasting? It is excluded…*" There can be no boasting or glorying in ourselves. Because we have **received** by faith the reconciliation, we can only glory in God.

Romans 5:1–11 sets forth nine benefits of justification by faith which is the foundation necessary for successful living.

Chapter 2
Doctrine of the Two Men

The first eleven verses of Romans five set forth the blessings that result from justification by faith. Verses 12–21 show the believer's former position compared to and contrasted with his present position, and it is preliminary to the doctrine of Sanctification. Before we can study this section, there are those areas of definition which we must consider.

Definition of Sin

In the first three chapters, unrighteousness and sins are described. Romans 1:18–3:20 prove conclusively the utter depravity of ALL mankind. These verses set forth the acts that result from a nature that is totally opposite from the nature of God. In verse 17, we see that the gospel sets forth the righteousness of God—there is nothing wrong with God in His character, His Person, or His actions.

In order to maintain balance, there must be a negative for every positive; therefore, if the gospel reveals the righteousness of God, it must also reveal the unrighteousness of man. In Romans 5:6, man is described as ungodly; in 5:8, we are described as sinners that carry out the acts of ungodliness. In verse 12, "sin" takes on a different meaning. In the previous citations, it refers to acts. From verse 12 through chapter 8, it refers to the principle that results in the acts. We see this clearly in I John 1:8–10:

*If we say that we have no sin, we deceive ourselves, and the truth is not in us. If we confess our sins, he is faithful and just to forgive us our sins, and to cleanse us from all unrighteousness. If we say that we have not **sinned**, we make him a liar, and his word is not in us.* (Emphasis mine)

In verse 8, sin is the root or nature, and in verses 9 and 10, sins and sinned is the fruit. This sin principle, or root, is called by different names in the New Testament: "the old man," "Adam," "the sin nature," and "the flesh" among others. It is unredeemable; it cannot be helpful and is always harmful. This does not mean that it cannot do good things, but it corrupts everything that it touches.

Paul said in Romans 7:18: *For I know that in me (that is in my flesh,) dwelleth no good thing.* The proof of that can be seen in the listing of the works of the flesh in Galatians 5:19–21.

We are told to "...*walk* (that is, live our lives) *in the Spirit* (or under the control of the Holy Spirit), *and you shall not fulfill the lust of the flesh: these are contrary the one to the other.*" The flesh, the sin nature, the old man, is the root out of which comes the fruit or actions that are sinful.

Definition of Death

Death is presented in two ways in the Bible—physical death as in Genesis 5 and spiritual death as in Ephesians

2:1: "*And you hath he quickened who were dead in trespasses and sins.*"

Since death is the absence of life, physical death is the absence of physical life, and spiritual death is the absence of spiritual life. When we are born, we are physically alive but spiritually dead.

Wherefore, as by one man sin entered into the world, and death by sin: and so death passed upon all men, for that all have sinned. Rom. 5:12

When Adam chose to disobey God, he came under the judgment pronounced by God in Genesis 2:17: "*...for in the day that thou eatest thereof, thou shalt surely die,*" and since all of mankind was in Adam, then all of mankind came under that sentence of death, both physical and spiritual.

For as in Adam all die, even so in Christ shall all be made alive. I Cor. 15:22

While a man may have physical life, he may not have spiritual life. If he dies physically while spiritually dead, the body will be placed in the grave, but the soul and spirit (the real person) goes to Hades, the place of conscious physical suffering for all eternity. On the other hand, when a physically alive, spiritually dead person receives, by faith alone, the finished work of Jesus Christ, he is made alive spiritually. Should he die physically in that state, his soul and spirit go immediately to Heaven to enjoy eternal bliss.

...I declare unto you the gospel...by which also ye are saved, ... how that Christ died for our sins according to the Scriptures;

and that he was buried, and that he rose again the third day...
I Cor. 15:1–4

We are confident, I say, and willing rather to be absent from the body, and to be present with the Lord. II Cor. 5:8

For to me to live is Christ and to die is gain. For I am in a strait betwixt two, having a desire to depart and to be with Christ, which is far better. Phil. 1:21, 23

Definition of Headship

Our understanding of the doctrine of Identification as set forth in Romans 6 depends on our understanding of headship. The Bible teaches that there are two heads of the human family, each with different consequences. By the federal, or representative, headship of Adam, we all stand condemned because we are in Adam by birth.

Wherefore, as by one man sin entered into the world, and death by sin: and so death passed upon all men, for that all have sinned. Rom. 5:12

According to Genesis 3:7, the first sin was disobedience to God committed by Adam and Eve in the garden. As a result, God pronounced death, both physical and spiritual, upon them and, through their leadership, the whole human race. By one man, Adam, the sin nature was imparted to all of mankind.

However, there is one alternative—the spiritual headship of Christ. The headship of Adam is by natural generation; the headship of Christ is by regeneration.

Jesus answered and said unto him, Verily, verily, I say unto thee, except a man be born again, (regeneration), *he cannot see the kingdom of God. Marvel not that I say unto thee, Ye must be born again* (regenerated). John 3:3–5

The federal headship of Adam results in condemnation and spiritual death, while the headship of Christ results in salvation and all the attendant blessings as we shall see in the following chapters.

Chapter 3
Doctrine of the Two Men Representatives

In the previous chapter, we laid some ground work necessary for us to understand God's plan for successful living. We looked at man as originally created, the fall and its consequences—spiritual and physical death for all since all were in the loins of Adam at the time of his sin. Therefore, all are born with the sin principle, or nature, which results in sinful practices.

Wherefore, as by one man sin entered into the world, and death by sin; and so death passed upon all men, for that all have sinned: (For until the law sin was in the world: but sin is not imputed when there is no law. Nevertheless death reigned from Adam to Moses, even over them that had not sinned after the similitude of Adam's transgression, who is the figure of him that was to come. But not as the offence, so also is the free gift. For if through the offence of one many be dead, much more the grace of God, and the gift by grace, which is by one man, Jesus Christ, hath abounded unto many. And not as it was by one that sinned, so is the gift: for the judgment was by one to condemnation, but the free gift is of many offences unto justification. For if by one man's offence death reigned by one; much more they which receive abundance of grace and of the gift of righteousness shall reign in life by one, Jesus Christ.) Therefore as by the offence of one judgment came upon all men to condemnation; even so by the righteousness of one the free gift came upon all men unto justification of life. For as by one man's disobedience many were made sinners, so by the obedience of one shall many be made righteous. Moreover the law entered, that the offence might abound. But where sin abounded, grace did much more abound: That as sin hath reigned unto death, even so might grace reign through righteousness unto eternal life by Jesus Christ our Lord. Rom. 5:12–21

We are now ready to look at the two representatives. The one representative is Adam, the head of the whole human race. Every human being is an offspring of Adam. As a representative, his acts involve all those connected with him by physical birth.

The other representative is Christ, Who is the Head of the heavenly family. As a representative, His acts involve all those who are connected with Him through regeneration.

As a human being, I was in Adam when he sinned; therefore, I am a partaker with him in his fall.

This is the book of the generations of Adam in the day that God created man in the likeness of God made he him. Gen. 5:1

Notice that man as originally created was in the likeness of God. That is, he had God's characteristics: life, personality, wisdom, and holiness. But after man exercised his free will and chose to disobey God, he was no longer in God's image, and his children were in his (Adam's) image.

And Adam lived an hundred and thirty years, and begat a son in his own likeness, after his image; and called his name Seth. Gen. 5:3

When I was born, I was not in Christ, nor was I in the image of God; but rather I was in the image and likeness of Adam and was, therefore, under the condemnation of death (Rom. 5:12).

To say I have never done anything wrong is to hide from the Biblical fact that is not what you do but what you are that condemns you.

For as in Adam all die, even so in Christ shall all be made alive. I Cor. 15:22

Even the moral man is condemned by the sin nature.

He that believeth on him is not condemned: but he that believeth not is condemned already, because he hath not believed in the name of the only begotten son of God. John 3:18

There are those who claim that they are not sinners because they keep the law. But that excuse is answered by the following verses from Romans 5:

For until the law sin was in the world: but sin is not imputed when there is no law. Nevertheless death reigned from Adam to Moses... (v. 13 & 14a)

The fact that people died from Adam until Moses gave the law is proof that in Adam all sin is under condemnation of God. If there is no law, it does not mean there is no sin; rather, because there was no law, sins were not changed, but sin (the nature) still reigned, and by that, death also reigned.

In verses 15–21, we see the two representatives compared and contrasted. In verses 15, 17, and 20, the work of Christ is compared to the work of Adam, and the work of Christ is greater than that of Adam.

In verses 18, 19, and 21, the work of Christ is contrasted with Adam's works, and the work of Christ is as deep as Adam's. We will look first at the contrast. In the first phrase of verse 18, we are told that by the offence of one, that is Adam (verse 12), judgment came upon all men and condemnation by that judgment. However, the second phrase in the verse is in contrast to the just: *"even so by the righteousness of one the free gift came upon all men unto justification of life."* By Adam's work, disobedience, all men were made sinners. By Christ's work, obedience unto death at the cross, all who are in Christ by faith in His finished work are justified or declared righteous.

For he (God) *hath made him* (Christ) *to be sin for us, who knew no sin: that we might be made the righteousness of God in him.* II Cor. 5:21

Then said he (Christ), *Lo, I come to do thy will, O God…By the which will we are sanctified through the offering of the body of Jesus Christ once for all.* Heb. 10:9a, 10

Christ's work of justification is just as deep as Adam's work of condemnation.

The contrast continues in verse 19. Here, there is contrast between the effect of Adam's disobedience. In Adam's disobedience, many were made sinners; in Christ's obedience, many are made righteous and have a right standing with God.

Let this mind be in you, which was also in Christ Jesus: Who, being in the form of God, thought it not robbery to be equal with God: But made himself of no reputation, and took upon him the form of a servant, and was made in the likeness of men: And being found in fashion as a man, he humbled himself, and became obedient unto death, even the death of the cross. Phil. 2:5–8

Christ's work of obedience is as deep as Adam's disobedience.

A third area of contrast is seen in verse 21, where we see the reign of the sin nature as contrasted with the reign of grace. When the sin nature received from Adam has rule in our lives, it results in death, while the grace of God's reign through the righteousness of Jesus Christ results in eternal life. Grace can only reign through righteousness imputed by Jesus Christ to those who place their faith in the finished work of Christ.

For the wages of sin is death; but the gift of God is eternal life through Jesus Christ our Lord. Rom. 6:23

Christ's work is at least as deep as Adam's, but if that were all that Christ did, then He is no better than Adam. He is just equal to Adam, but opposite. However, God is greater, and Christ's work is greater. We can see that when we compare Adam with Christ in verses 17, 20, and 21.

Notice the "much more" in the verses. It is a comparative term, and it is a superlative. God's grace in Christ exceeds Adam's offence, therefore, there is no offence or sin that is greater than God's grace.

In verse 17, we see that Adam's offence results in spiritual death ruling in man, but "much more," God's grace and righteousness results in the spiritual life ruling. This does not apply only to the lost, but it also applies to those who have experienced the grace of God. When Adam rules in our lives, that is death, and we do not experience successful living.

No matter the depth of the sin of Adam, in which we participated by virtue of being in Adam, whose nature we still have, God's grace goes beyond that, and not only saves us but also gives us the ability to live successfully.

Perhaps the following chart of verses 15–21 will help to visualize the comparisons and the contrasts:

In Christ	Verse	In Adam
Grace	15	Offense: death
Justification	16	Sin and judgment
Reign in life	17	Reign of death
Righteousness: life	18	Judgment and condemnation
Obedience	19	Disobedience
Abounding grace	20	Abounding sin
Eternal life	21	Eternal death

Chapter 4
The Meaning of Baptism

What shall we say then? Shall we continue in sin that grace may abound? God forbid. How shall we, that are dead to sin, live any longer therein? Know ye not, that so many of us as were baptized into Jesus Christ were baptized into his death? Therefore we are buried with him by baptism into death: that like as Christ was raised up from the dead by the glory of the Father, even so we also should walk in newness of life. Rom. 6:1–4

It is clear from Romans chapters 6–8 that salvation involved more than just being saved from the penalty of sin and the promise of a home in Heaven at the end of this life. God has a wonderful plan for each of His children to live a life of abundant blessing and fruitfulness.

The person who professes to know Christ as Savior, who actively or passively rebels against the Word of God, who experiences cycles of depression and rejoicing (but only gets a blessing on Sunday morning), is living under the power of the old sin nature. That is not what Jesus intended when He said:

The thief cometh not but for to steal, and to kill, and to destroy: I am come that they might have life, and that they might have it more abundantly. John 10:10

Success in the Christian life from God's point of view is not an accident but a direct result of living in harmony with Biblical principles. The average Christian today is not experiencing a meaningful life but rather one of conflict in nearly every area. This is due to one of two reasons: ignorance of Biblical principles or abstinence in applying the Biblical principles to life. It is hoped that this book will solve the first one. The second one can only be solved as you respond positively to the promptings of the Holy Spirit.

The last phrase of Romans 5:20 says: *"But where sin abounded, grace did much more abound."* This statement obviously gives rise to the human rationalization that if we want more grace, we should sin more. The thinking goes, "Since sin abounding results in grace abounding, let's continue in sin so we have more grace." That is 6:1. But the Holy Spirit answers in verse 2: *"God forbid."* Then follows a rhetorical question: *"How shall we that are dead to sin, live any longer therein?"* The Greek verb for *dead* is in the aorist tense. That is, it is done. It is not that we are dying or that we shall die to sin's control, but we have already died to its control, and that is the state in which we continue. We have died; we are already dead to the control of the sin nature. The sin nature is not dead, but we are dead to its control. It is not something that is happening, nor is it something that is going to happen, nor is it something we must do. It is something that is done, and we simply accept it by faith. The word *"dead"* in verse 2 refers to the effect produced by death, not a process.

Wherefore if ye be dead with Christ from the rudiments of the world,... Col. 2:20a

The word "if" is a first class condition in the Greek and can be translated "since." It is a statement of fact. This is borne out in Colossians 3:3: *"For ye are dead and your life is hid with Christ in God."* How did that happen?

Know ye not, that so many of us as were baptized into Jesus Christ were baptized into his death? Rom. 6:3

The word "baptize" means "to immerse or to place into." The moment an individual believes the gospel and trusts Christ as his or her Savior, the Holy Spirit baptizes or places that person into Christ.

For by one Spirit are we all baptized into one body, whether we be Jews or Gentiles, whether we be bond or free: and have been all made to drink into one Spirit. I Cor. 12:13

For we are his workmanship, created in Christ Jesus unto good works, which God hath before ordained that we should walk in them. Eph. 2:10

But now in Christ Jesus ye who sometimes were far off are made nigh by the blood of Christ. Eph. 2:13

Being baptized into Christ identifies us with Christ in His death, burial, and resurrection. Not only were we placed in Christ, but He was placed in us by His Holy Spirit.

Know ye not that ye are the temple of God, and that the Spirit of God dwelleth in you? I Cor. 3:16

*What? Know ye not that your body is the temple of the Holy Ghost which is **in** you, which ye have of God, and ye are not your own?* I Cor. 6:19

*…which is Christ **in** you the hope of glory.* Col. 1:27

*Whereby are given unto us exceeding great and precious promises: that by these ye might be **partakers** of the divine nature…* II Pet. 1:4a

The believer is in Christ, and Christ is in the believer. Being baptized, placed in Christ, by the Holy Spirit, we become one with Him, and we are partakers of all things of which He partook. Positionally, we were crucified; therefore, we are dead to the sin nature's control. Practically, we are alive, and the sin nature is in conflict with the new nature.

This I say then, walk in the Spirit, and ye shall not fulfill the lust of the flesh. For the flesh lusteth against the Spirit, and the Spirit against the flesh: and these are contrary the one to the other: so that ye cannot do the things that ye would. Gal. 5:16–17

There is, therefore, a struggle within for control. We will see that conflict when we come to Romans chapter 7.

While verse 3 speaks of the Holy Spirit's baptism into Christ, verse 4 speaks of water baptism as a picture of the baptism. Just as the Holy Spirit placed the believer into Christ, so the believer is placed into the water. That is why we do not sprinkle. That is why we do not baptize unbelievers. Water baptism is a symbol, a picture of our identification with Christ. Water baptism does not save, does not help save, does not keep one saved, does not equip one for successful living, does not make one a Baptist or make one a church member. It is only a testimony, and that is why every person who trusts Christ should be baptized. It is the outward manifestation of the inward work of the Holy Spirit. Therefore, our testimony at water baptism should be:

I turn my back on the old life;

I renounce forever the old ways;

I know my old man was crucified;

Now, by this act, I indicate the burial of the old man and my resurrection to new life in Christ.

Many of us ask for more power to overcome the old man, but as we shall see in the next chapter, he is already dead. The conflict is over, and we are the victors in and through Christ.

Chapter 5
Knowing

There are two vital biblical truths that are essential to living successfully:

1. Living in victory over the practice of sin

2. The complete control of the Holy Spirit in our lives

These are actually related, but we want to separate them in the next three chapters. These truths are spelled out in three words. The first word is "knowing" in verses 6–10:

Knowing this, that our old man is crucified with him, that the body of sin might be destroyed, that henceforth we should not serve sin. For he that is dead is freed from sin. Now if we be dead with Christ, we believe that we shall also live with him: Knowing that Christ being raised from the dead dieth no more; death hath no more dominion over him. For in that he died, he died unto sin once: but in that he liveth, he liveth unto God.

This word "knowing" has the idea of "knowing in yourself." It is a knowledge that goes beyond a mere mental assent to facts. The facts were given to us in verses 1–4:

Verse 2: we are dead to the sin nature's control.

Verse 3: this tells us how that happened—we became identified (by the baptism of the Holy Spirit) with Christ in all that He did, that is His death, burial, and resurrection.

When He died, we died; when He arose, we arose. God did not change the old man, rather He took it to the cross in Christ.

I am crucified with Christ: nevertheless I live; yet not I, but Christ liveth in me: and the life which I now live in the flesh I live by the faith of the Son of God, who loved me, and gave himself for me. Gal. 2:20

For ye are dead, and your life is hid with Christ in God. Col. 3:3

On the cross, Christ was made to be what we are, that we might become in Him what He is.

For he hath made him to be sin for us, who knew no sin; that we might be made the righteousness of God in him. II Cor. 5:21

And you hath he quickened who were dead in trespasses and sins. Eph. 2:1

Who his own self bare our sins in his own body on the tree, that we, being dead to sins, should live unto righteousness: by whose stripes ye were healed. I Pet. 2:24

This "knowing" is to become convinced thoroughly of these facts. If you are going to be free from the bondage of sin, you must allow the Holy Spirit through the Word of God to convince you that your old man is dead.

We do not like to admit that. Rather, we like to think there is still something of value in that old man. After all, we have a great personality, we have talent, we have training. Surely God can use us!

God says NO!

For I know that in me (that is, in my flesh,) dwelleth no good thing: for to will is present with me; but how to perform that which is good I find not.

Romans 6:6 says our old man was crucified…

"…*that*…" for a purpose,

"…*the body of sin*…" that is the root which brings forth the fruit,

"…*might be destroyed*…" this is not and cannot be referring to the physical life, but to the old sin nature being put to death.

"…*that henceforth we should not serve sin.*" From this point on, (actually, from the point of our salvation) we are freed from the power or control of the sin nature. That being the case, we do not need to serve sin, because our old sin nature is dead to the allurements of sin. That is not to say we cannot sin, because we can and we do, but we do not have to sin.

Our breathing is a good illustration of this. We normally inhale and exhale fourteen times every minute. We must do it, we are in bondage to it. But if I die, there are no more inhales or exhales. My bondage to breathing is ended. The same thing is true spiritually. I am dead to the sin nature's control.

Some may say, "But I don't feel dead. I don't act it. I still yield to sin." God says you are dead (Col. 3:3). If God says you are dead, you are whether you feel it or not. It is like salvation. Do you feel saved? No, but you base your salvation on God's Word. Look back at verse 3: *"Know ye not, that so many of us were baptized into Jesus Christ* (at salvation) *were baptized into his death?"* It is a finished work—you are dead. Verse 8 says, *"Now if* (since) *we be dead with Christ...."* This verse does not say "we might be" or "we shall be;" it simply states a fact that is true. It is done!

Verse 10 says that when Christ died, He died to sin once. That is, His relationship to sin was finished, and He need not die again, need not be made sin again (II Cor. 5:21) because He died to it. The same is true for us.

When we trusted Christ as Savior, we became identified with Him in His death. Sin has no more dominion or rule over us. This identification with Him is not only negative death, by it is also positive—that is, alive with Him!

Knowing that Christ being raised from the dead dieth no more; death hath no more dominion over him. Rom. 6:9

Identification with Christ means we share His death and His life. That is His resurrection life. Just as He died unto sin and lives unto God, so it is with those who are identified with Him.

It is a faithful saying: For if we be dead with him, we shall also live with him: II Tim. 2:11

...that we might be made the righteousness of God in him.
II Cor. 5:21b

Who his own self bare our sins in his own body on the tree, that we, being dead to sins, should live unto righteousness: by whose stripes ye were healed. I Pet. 2:24

So many of us are living defeated lives—saved and giving lip-service to the resurrection but knowing nothing of the resurrected life.

The fact of God is that when I trusted Christ as Savior, the Holy Spirit put me into Christ and all that He is. My old man was crucified with Him; I was buried with Him; I was raised with Him to newness of life. The question is: how can this be real in my life on a regular basis? That is covered by the next word we will consider.

Chapter 6
Reckoning

Likewise reckon ye also yourselves to be dead indeed unto sin, but alive unto God through Jesus Christ our Lord. Rom. 6:11

We ended the last chapter with a question. My old man was crucified with Him; I was buried with Him; I was raised to newness of life with Him. How can this be real in my life on a regular basis?

On the cross, Christ was made to be what we were in order that we might be made what He is, that is the righteousness of God.

For he hath made him to be sin for us, who knew no sin; that we might be made the righteousness of God in him. II Cor. 5:21

God did not change the old man, but sent it to the cross to release us from its control. Again, the question—How? Verse 11 starts with the word "likewise," (even so, in the same way), takes us back to verse 10, which says Christ died to sin's dominion once, but now lives unto the end. This gives rise to a series of rhetorical questions:

Did Christ die to sin's dominion? Yes.

How many times? Once.

Was He raised from the dead? Yes.

Unto Whom does He now live? God.

Have you received Christ as Savior?

If so, where are you today? The answer to this is found in Ephesians 1:3,4,6,7 for starters.

Therefore, when Christ died, you died; but since you are in Him, you also now live in Him. The life which you now live, you live by the faith of the Son of God. How do you make this real in your life? By *reckoning*. The word means "to impute, or count, what Christ did and is as your own." Perhaps the best illustration of this is in Paul's letter to Philemon on behalf of Onesimus, when he tells Philemon in verse 18: *"If he hath wronged thee, or oweth thee ought, put that on my account,"* or "charge that to me."

In Romans 4:4–6 and 8–11, when Abraham believed God, it (his faith) was counted for righteousness. The same is true for the victory over sin in your life. You simply believe that when Christ died to sin's dominion, you died to sin's dominion because you are in Him by faith. Faith is my acceptance of God's fact, whatever that may be, whether it is the forgiveness of sins or victorious living.

Now faith is the substance of things hoped for, the evidence of things not seen. Heb. 11:1

Are you saved because God said so? NO! You are saved because God said so, and you believed what God said! You have accepted that truth as yours by faith. You reckoned Christ's payment for sin as yours, and you are free from the penalty of sin. You do not tell yourself all day that you are saved. You do not ask God to save you each day many times. You simply rest in the fact that God said it, and you believe it. You count it or reckon it as yours and rest in God's Word.

The same is true concerning our death to sin's control. We are not called upon to die, we are already dead.

God forbid. How shall we, that are dead to sin, live any longer therein? Rom. 6:2

For ye are dead, and your life is hid with Christ in God. Col. 3:3

I am crucified with Christ: nevertheless I live; yet not I, but Christ liveth in me: and the life which I now live in the flesh I live by the faith of the Son of God, who loved me, and gave himself for me. Gal. 2:20

What about I Corinthians 15:21 where Paul says, *"…I die daily…"*? It is obvious from Romans 6 that he is reckoning by faith the fact of his identification with Christ in His death. That is what Jesus is saying in Luke 9:23: *"And he said to them all, If any man will come after me, let him deny himself, and take up his cross daily, and follow me."* Faith is active, not a one-time crisis experience.

We are called upon to count or impute to ourselves something that is already done. Only as we claim, by faith, the completed action of our death, burial, and resurrection with Christ can Romans 6:14 be true in our lives: *"For sin shall not have dominion over you: for ye are not under the law, but under grace."*

This is a promise, but notice it does not say "sin cannot" but rather "sin shall not." If we forget or fail to reckon on our position in Christ, the old sin nature exercises its dominion over us once again, and many people are in bondage to the sin nature but do not need to be.

We simply need to accept by faith the fact that we are dead to sin's control and thank God for it.

But that no man is justified by the law in the sight of God, it is evident: for, The just shall live by faith. Gal. 3:11

It is simply a matter of saying, "I am crucified with Christ, thank You, Lord, the power of sin is broken!" This is best seen in Col. 2:6: *"As ye have therefore received Christ Jesus the Lord, so walk ye in him:"* and in Gal. 5:25: *"If we live in the Spirit, let us also walk in the Spirit."*

Chapter 7
Yield

Neither yield ye your members as instruments of unrighteousness unto sin: but yield yourselves unto God, as those that are alive from the dead, and your members as instruments of righteousness unto God. Rom. 6:13

In Romans 6:6, we are given the fact of our identification with Christ in His death, burial, and resurrection. Verse 11 then tells that fact must be appropriated by faith. We simply need to accept, by faith, the fact that upon being baptized by the Holy Spirit into Christ, we died with Him, and we are, therefore, dead to the old sin nature's control. The life of victory is simply a matter of believing the facts of God. Some thoughts from the epistle to the Galatians will be helpful here.

Galatians was written to correct two errors:

1. Justification by the works of the law which is dealt with in 2:16: *Knowing that a man is not justified by the works of the law, but by the faith of Jesus Christ, even we have believed in Jesus Christ, that we might be justified by the faith of Christ, and not by the works of the law: for by the works of the law shall no flesh be justified.* and 3:11: *But that no man is justified by the law in the sight of God, it is evident: for, The just shall live by faith.*

2. Victory over sin by works, (do this, don't do that) which is dealt with in 3:1–3: *O foolish Galatians, who hath bewitched you, that ye should not obey the truth, before whose eyes Jesus Christ hath been evidently set forth, crucified among you? This only would I learn of you, Received ye the Spirit by the works of the law, or by the hearing of faith? Are ye so foolish? having begun in the Spirit, are ye now made perfect by the flesh?*

Here, Paul asks the question: "How did you get saved, by works or by faith?" The answer, of course, is by faith. He then goes on to show them that having been saved by faith, their spiritual growth and victory over sin are accomplished in the same way. He goes on to emphasize this in 5:25: *If we live in the Spirit, let us also walk in the Spirit.*

Victory over the sin nature, spiritual maturity, is obtained in the same way as salvation, that is, by faith.

As ye have therefore received Christ Jesus the Lord, so walk ye in him. Col. 2:6

"I am crucified with Christ." Thank You, Lord, the power of sin is broken! Rom. 6:14

Many Christians *know* and *reckon*, but they still have failures in their walk with the Lord. Why? The question brings us to the third word in Romans 6 which is necessary to our Christian walk, *yield*. Genuine victorious living comes from all three of these words. All three of them must be true in our lives. We need to look at this word "yield" in three different areas.

I. The Meaning of the Word—II Chron. 30:8

The word "yield" here is from the Hebrew word "yad" which means "to give the hand." It has the idea in the context of submission to God. The idea is to hold yourself in an open hand to God, not grasping or holding back on Him. The same idea is seen in Romans 6:13,16,19; 12:1. In these verses, the meaning is "to be at hand; standing by; being available," that is, to be totally available to God.

In verse 13, it is both negative, *"neither yield ye your members,"* and positive, *"but yield your members."* In the second or positive use, it is in the present tense, that is, "be presenting" as a continuous action. We are to be habitually submitting ourselves with "open hands" to God.

II. The Mechanics of Yielding—Rom. 6:12–19

As we have already seen, they are both positive and negative. Negatively—verse 12—*"Let not...."* in other words, it is up to us. II Chronicles 30:8 says, *"...be ye not stiffnecked...."* The responsibility for submission is ours. We are to voluntarily submit ourselves to God and not resist His will. The first phrase of verse 13 says, "Don't yield, don't make your members available to be instruments of unrighteousness." Our members—eyes, ears, mouth, hands, feet, mind—are all in contact with the world system, and we must be constantly on our guard, lest it invades us through our yielding to it. When we make our members available (yield) to the world system, the old sin nature is ready to assume control. When the natural desires are yielded to in self-will or self-indulgence, the sin nature uses these desires to assert its authority and establish its reign; therefore, **don't yeld!** Starve the old man.

But put ye on the Lord Jesus Christ, and make not provision for the flesh, to fulfil the lusts thereof. Rom. 13:14

Abstain from all appearance of evil. I Thess. 5:22

For the flesh lusteth against the Spirit, and the Spirit against the flesh: and these are contrary the one to the other: so that ye cannot do the things that ye would. Gal. 5:22

Dearly beloved, I beseech you as strangers and pilgrims, abstain from fleshly lusts, which war against the soul. I Pet. 2:11

The second phrase of verse 13 sets forth the positive aspect of yielding: *"...but yield yourselves to God as those that are alive from the dead, and your members as instruments of righteousness unto God."* Remember Galatians 2:20—I have been crucified with Christ, therefore, I am dead, but I am alive. The old life no longer controls, but the resurrection life of Christ does! Therefore, I am to yield my members as instruments of righteousness, all of my members—eyes, ears, mouth, feet, etc.

Think back to when you were saved. (I Cor. 12,13) The testimony of that baptism is water baptism. Did all of you (your members) go under? Then you are to turn over complete control of **all** of you to the indwelling Holy Spirit.

Know ye not, that to whom ye yield yourselves servants to obey, his servants ye are to whom ye obey; whether of sin unto death, or of obedience unto righteousness? I speak after the manner of men because of the infirmity of your flesh: for as ye have yielded your members servants to uncleanness and to iniquity unto iniquity; even so now yield your members servants to righteousness unto holiness. Rom. 6:16,19

To illustrate, a pen can be used to write a gospel song or tract or a pornographic piece of literature. It depends upon to whom it is yielded. A pen cannot make a choice, unlike you and I, who can choose to whom we yield. This is not a one-time crisis decision like salvation or surrender for service, although, there may need to be an initial crisis experience. There must be a continual reckoning by faith and conscious yielding of all to God and then living under the control of the Holy Spirit.

For which cause we faint not; but though our outward man perish, yet the inward man is renewed day by day. II Cor. 4:16

I protest by your rejoicing which I have in Christ Jesus our Lord, I die daily. I Cor. 15:31

III. Practical Application

We all know the meaning of the highway "yield" sign: "to give the right of way to another." In our spiritual journey, we come upon many of these signs as God deals with us about different matters in our lives. We are, therefore, to yield the right of way in our lives to Another, even Jesus Christ.

We are to hold all we are and all we have in our open hands to God. Our members, ourselves, our goals, our plans, our rights, our spouses, our children—anything and everything that God calls for must be yielded if we are going to have victory.

Chapter 8
Christian Liberty

In the previous chapters, we have seen that we have been identified with Christ in His death, burial, and resurrection, and therefore, we took part of the same. We no longer need to be under the power of the sin nature. We are to count that truth as ours by faith, and we are to yield ourselves to God. All of this is the work of God on our behalf in Christ; it is all of grace. It is not what we can do, it is what Christ *has done*!

The first part of Romans 6:14 tells us that *"sin shall not have dominion (or rule) over (us)."* The second part tells us why: *"for you are not under the law, but under grace."*

There are and have been those who have taken this to mean that once we are saved, we can keep on sinning without any consequences. However, verse 15 warns against the abuse of that liberty: *"What then? Shall we sin, because we are not under the law, but under grace? God forbid."* This question is distinct from the one in verse 1. There, the question is, *"Shall we continue in sin…,"* that is, under the control of the sin nature. Here, the question is, *"Shall we sin…,"* that is, commit acts of sin. The answer to the first question is, *"God forbid."* because by identification with Christ, the power of the sin nature was broken, and we are free. The answer to the second question is the same as the answer to the first: *"God forbid"* because we are set free to serve Him. This second answer is developed in verses 16–23, where we have a two-fold reason why we should not sin.

I. We are in bondage to whomever we obey.

Eight times in these verses, the word *servant* is found. In each case, it is the Greek word for bondslave. There are two words translated *servant*—in one, the servant serves, but ownership is not passed, that is, there is no bondage; in the other, the servant is owned by the master. This is the word that is translated *servant* in these verses. There can only be one of two masters for the Christian—God or sin. We are the slave of one or the other. Jesus said, *"No man can serve two masters: for either he will hate the one, and love the other; or else he will hold to the one, and despise the other. Ye cannot serve God and mammon"* (Matt. 6:24).

Paul said, *"For we know that the law is spiritual: but I am carnal, sold under sin."* (Rom. 7:14) That indicates ownership, but in I Corinthians 6:19–20: *"What? Know ye not that your body is the temple of the Holy Ghost which is in you, which ye have of God, and ye are not your own? For ye are bought with a price: therefore glorify God in your body, and in your spirit, which are God's."* We are owned by Christ. He bought us; therefore, we are to place ourselves in bondage to Him.

Verse 17 tells us that we "were the slaves of sin." That is, we were in bondage to the sin nature. That is what we were, but that is no longer true. The chains of bondage to sin were broken at the Cross because we "obeyed from the heart that form of doctrine which has delivered you." We obeyed by believing (Acts 16:31) and by calling (Rom. 10:13).

In verse 18, we see the results of being made free from sin. By the very act of believing and calling, we became slaves of righteousness, therefore, of God. What a difference from our former position as slaves of sin! According to verse 21, all we could expect from our bondage to sin was shame and death, but we can expect blessing and freedom in our bondage to righteousness.

The fruit of this freedom can be seen in verses 19–22. Verse 19 says that in the same way we yielded our members to the sin nature, now we are to yield our members to the divine nature that dwells in us (II Pet. 1:4). When we were in bondage to sin, we fed the old sin nature on the things of this world, the flesh, and the devil. We ignored the things of God and sought the things of the flesh. These were not necessarily bad things. It is entirely possible to be involved in preaching, teaching a Sunday school class, passing out tracts, even going to a foreign mission field in the flesh. Just as we fed the old nature, we are now to yield to God and feed the new nature with Bible study, prayer, fellowship with other believers, and submission to the indwelling of the Holy Spirit of God. Before we were saved, we had no righteousness (v. 20) which resulted in the fruit of sins described in I Cor. 6:9–11:

Know ye not that the unrighteous shall not inherit the kingdom of God? Be not deceived: neither fornicators, nor idolaters, nor adulterers, nor effeminate, nor abusers of themselves with mankind, Nor thieves, nor covetous, nor drunkards, nor revilers, nor extortioners, shall inherit the kingdom of God. And such were some of you: but ye are washed, but ye are sanctified, but ye are justified in the name of the Lord Jesus, and by the Spirit of our God.

Notice "such **were** some of you." That is past tense. That is what we were as servants of sin, but now we are set free from that bondage and are become servants of righteousness. Result? The fruit of holiness and freedom.

Does this mean we can live any way we please? No! To continue in known sin can result in physical death (verse 23).

If any man see his brother sin a sin which is not unto death, he shall ask, and he shall give him life for them that sin not unto death. There is a sin unto death: I do not say that he shall pray for it. I John 5:16

For he that eateth and drinketh unworthily, eateth and drinketh damnation to himself, not discerning the Lord's body. For this cause many are weak and sickly among you, and many sleep. I Cor. 11:29–30

But a certain man named Ananias, with Sapphira his wife, sold a possession, and kept back part of the price, his wife also being privy to it, and brought a certain part, and laid it at the apostles' feet. But Peter said, Ananias, why hath Satan filled thine heart to lie to the Holy Ghost, and to keep back part of the price of the land? Whiles it remained, was it not thine own? And after it was sold, was it not in thine own power? Why has thou conceived this thing in thine heart? Thou has not lied unto men, but unto God. And Ananias hearing these words fell down, and gave up the ghost: and great fear came on all them that heard these things. Acts 5:1–5

What then are we to do?

1. Keep short accounts—I Jn. 1:9
   Confess sin as soon as it is committed.

2. Practice prevention—I Jn. 1:7
   Yield to God and feed on the things of God. Then keep walking in God.

While the primary interpretation of Romans 6:23 is to Christians, this verse must also be understood to speak to those who are lost. For all that sin will ever bring is death, both physical and spiritual. Death is the wages of sin, while eternal life is the free gift of God.

Wherefore, as by one man sin entered into the world, and death by sin; and so death passed upon all men, for that all have sinned. Rom. 5:12

And you hath he quickened, who were dead in trespasses and sins. Eph. 2:1

In order for sinful man to have life, God in the Person of His Son Jesus Christ had to die.

Moreover, brethren, I declare unto you the gospel which I preached unto you, which also ye have received, and wherein ye stand; By which also ye are saved, if ye keep in memory what I preached unto you, unless ye have believed in vain. For I delivered unto you first of all that which I also received, how that Christ died for our sins according to the scriptures; and that he was buried, and that he rose again the third day according to the scriptures. I Cor. 15:1–4

If you are lost, you must receive this gift before it is too late.

But as many as received him, to them gave he power to become the sons of God, even to them that believe on his name. Jn. 1:12

Dear Christian friend, you are slave to one of the following—sin or righteousness. Which one?

Chapter 9
The Conflict of the Ages

Alva J. McClain wrote in his commentary on Romans: "However difficult the seventh chapter of Romans may be, no trouble will be encountered whatever if we have actually mastered what the sixth chapter has taught." That is our identification with Christ in His death, burial, and resurrection.

The normal Christian life or the successful life from God's point of view is supernatural. This life is the life of the Lord Jesus lived out in our humanity, not by our self-effort or by invitation but by the indwelling Holy Spirit as we yield to Him.

In Philippians 2:3–8, we see the supernatural life, as lived out by the Lord Jesus in His self-humbling to be our Savior. It is natural for us to seek our own glory, to puff up our own reputation, to be served rather than to serve, to be proud, to be disobedient, but that is not the supernatural life of the Lord Jesus. All these actions in verses 3–8 were characteristics of the Lord Jesus, so if I am allowing the Holy Spirit to live out the life of the Lord Jesus in my daily walk, none of these "natural" things will be true. Therefore, if we are to live a consistent, successful life, we must remember that our only responsibility is to be submissive to the complete control of the indwelling Holy Spirit. When we do not submit, then no matter how much we may reckon on the facts of Romans 6, the conflict of Romans 7:15–25 is going to be true in our lives:

For that which I do I allow not: for what I would, that do I not; but what I hate, that do I. If then I do that which I would not, I consent unto the law that it is good. Now then it is no more I that do it, but sin that dwelleth in me. For I know that in me (that is, in my flesh,) dwelleth no good thing: for to will is present with me; but how to perform that which is good I find not. For the good that I would I do not: but the evil which I would not, that I do. Now if I do that I would not, it is no more I that do it, but sin that dwelleth in me. I find then a law, that, when I would do good, evil is present with me. For I delight in the law of God after the inward man: But I see another law in my members, warring against the law of my mind, and bringing me into captivity to the law of sin which is in my members. O wretched man that I am! who shall deliver me from the body of this death? I thank God through Jesus Christ our Lord. So then with the mind I myself serve the law of God; but with the flesh the law of sin.

This section of Romans 7 is autobiographical. It was the real experience of Paul after he was saved and after the revelations God had given him in his Arabian desert experience, and it is the experience of many of God's people who know the Word and may even be serving Him with all the energy they can muster, but still fail. Why? It is a part of human nature to do something for someone who has done something for us. So it is with God. Our natural attitude is, "He's done so much for me, I must do something for Him!" We start and fail and have Paul's experience as recorded in the verses above.

To get the complete context of this experience, we must start in verse 12: *"Wherefore the law is holy, and the commandment holy, and just, and good."* There is nothing wrong with the law, but it was not given to make us good, but rather to show us how bad we were and the impossibility of our keeping it. We try anyways and fail. Verse 14 says that the law is spiritual, but I am carnal, fleshly, and under the control of the sin nature. Just as we could not be saved by keeping the law, so we cannot live in victory by keeping the law. Every child of God has two natures. One is the nature with which we were born, that is the Adamic nature which cannot and does not receive the things of God (I Cor. 2:14); it cannot be changed (Rom.8:7). It is under the sentence of death (I Cor.15:22).

The other is the divine nature, received at the moment of salvation (II Pet. 1:4).

Jesus answered, Verily, verily, I say unto you, Except a man be born of water and of the Spirit, he cannot enter into the kingdom of God. Jn. 3:5

To whom God would make known what is the riches of the glory of this mystery among the Gentiles; which is Christ in you, the hope of glory. Col. 1:27

This nature is diametrically opposed to the old nature. These are the two "I's" of verses 15–25.

This I say then, Walk in the Spirit, and ye shall not fulfil the lust of the flesh. For the flesh lusteth against the Spirit, and the Spirit against the flesh: and these are contrary the one to the other: so that ye cannot do the things that ye would. If we live in the Spirit, let us also walk in the Spirit. Gal. 5:16,17,25

Notice especially verse 17: *"For the flesh lusteth against the Spirit, and the Spirit against the flesh...."* What follows is a long list of works of the flesh. These works of the flesh are a result of self-effort.

In contrast, verse 22 lists the nine-fold fruit of the Spirit. These are not the result of "I" bringing forth fruit, for "I" can not. Fruit comes without any self-effort. If I want to have tomatoes, I can only plant the roots and let them produce the fruit. As we live our lives under the control of the indwelling Holy Spirit, we will find that our lives and actions are pleasing to God and ourselves, and we will not experience the frustration that is set forth in Romans 7.

A good illustration of this conflict is seen in the Old Testament people known as the Amalekites. In I Samuel 15, Saul was ordered by God to totally destroy the Amalekites:

Thus saith the LORD of hosts, I remember that which Amalek did to Israel, how he laid wait for him in the way, when he came up from Egypt. Now go and smite Amalek, and utterly destroy all that they have, and spare them not; but slay both man and woman, infant and suckling, ox and sheep, camel and ass.
I Sam. 15:2–3

Who are these people, and why does God want them destroyed? Genesis 36:12 tells us that Amalek was Esau's grandson. We know from Genesis 25:30–34 that Esau was only interested in the things of the flesh, and that characteristic was passed down to his grandson. We find that Amalek was always in conflict with the people of God. Thus, Amalek becomes a type of the flesh always in conflict with the Spirit.

Remember what Amalek did unto thee by the way, when ye were come forth out of Egypt; How he met thee by the way, and smote the hindmost of thee, even all that were feeble behind thee, when thou was faint and weary; and he feared not God. Therefore it shall be, when the LORD thy God hath given thee rest from all thine enemies round about, in the land which the LORD thy God giveth thee for an inheritance to possess it, that thou shalt blot out the remembrance of Amalek from under heaven; thou shalt not forget it. Deut. 25:17–19

In these verses, we see how Amalek works. He "smote the hindmost, the feeble, and the faint," and that is precisely how the flesh, the Adamic nature, works. It attacks us at our weakest places and defeats us.

In Romans 7:17, Paul says that in his flesh he does not have the ability to live the Christian life. While he has the will or desire to do so, he cannot. He says, "I know what I ought to do and I want to it, but I don't have the power to do it." Notice Exodus 17:14–16: *"And the Lord said unto Moses, Write this for a memorial in a book, and rehearse it in the ears of Joshua: for I will utterly put out the remembrance of Amalek from under heaven. And Moses built an altar, and called the name of it Jehovah-nissi: For he said, Because the Lord hath sworn that the Lord will have war with Amalek from generation to generation."*

God will have war with Amalek from generation to generation. It is God's responsibility to defeat the flesh and live out the Christian life. This is what Paul wanted, but it eluded him until he came to the end of himself. In verses 15–23, we see his continual conflict between the flesh and the Spirit until finally, he comes to the end of himself, and in verse 24 cries out, *"O wretched man that I am! Who shall deliver me from the body of this death?"* It was then that he realized that victory was not something that he could achieve by self-effort, but that victory was his as he trusted Jesus Christ's finished work. Verse 25a: *"I thank God through Jesus Christ our Lord."*

Paul's experience is undoubtedly shared by multitudes of Christians reading these words. Everything seems to be going fine, but there is a hunger, a gnawing, a desire for something better than the humdrum existence of just getting by in the Christian life. You are working at what you think a Christian ought to be, and you fail miserably.

Someday God is going to bring you to a place where you have no answers, where your life is a total failure, where you can do nothing but realize what you are and admit to God, "O wretched man (or woman) that I am, I can't—You can! Thank you!"

That is victory! That is the life of faith, a life of "thank you" and not "please."

Chapter 10
Two Laws

Romans chapter 6 sets forth the "How" of the victorious Christian life—identification with Christ in His death, burial, and resurrection. Chapter 7 shows the utter futility of trying to live that life by the flesh—we try and fail and try again to no avail.

Chapter 8 shows the provision God has made for every Christian to live that life all the time. We concluded the last chapter with that great declaration of faith. *"I thank God through Jesus Christ our Lord."* (Rom. 7:25a)

Chapter 8 opens with a look back. "Therefore" looks back to that great shout of victory at the end of chapter 7.

In chapter 7, Paul was condemning himself for his failures in verses 15–17, then in verse 24, the cry of despair: *"O wretched man that I am...,"* followed by the realization that the answer was not in himself, but rather in the indwelling Lord Jesus Christ. Only the Lord Jesus Christ can deliver us from the condemnation we all desire. This is clearly set forth in the first verse of chapter 8.

In verse 2, there are two laws set forth: the law of the Spirit of life in Christ in which the Apostle delights according to Romans 7:22, and the law of sin and death from which we have been set free by the law of the Spirit of life. A law is a principle that happens the same all the time, for example the Law of Gravity. Every time we drop a book or a cup or even a piece of paper, the Law of Gravity takes over, and whatever we drop falls to the ground. That is the Law of Gravity, and it happens every time except when that law is superseded or overcome by another law. A jetliner is held on the ground by the Law of Gravity until the Law of Aerodynamics takes over, then that plane and everyone in it overcomes the Law of Gravity. As long as we stay in the plane, we enjoy victory over the Law of Gravity.

That is the principle that is set forth in verses 2–4. The Christian has a desire to live right, to act right, and to serve God just as Paul did in Romans 7:15–20. So often that desire motivates us to live that life in our own strength, but the law of sin in our members (7:23) overcomes us, defeats us, and it always will. It is a law! It happens every time! Let's see how this works.

The Mosaic Law, the moral code, says, *"Thou shalt not commit adultery."* Jesus set forth the real intent of that when He said, *"...whosoever looketh on a woman to lust after her hath committed adultery with her already in his heart"* (Matt. 5:28). How does this work? A young lady walks by dressed in the attire of an harlot and you look. With the law of sin, that look sets in motion an evil thought process that results in fantasizing an action in your mind. That is adultery. Every time you see, you think, and you sin. However, you do not want to do that! How can you overcome? The bad news is that you can not; the good news is Jesus can! How? We need to go back to chapter 6:13–20. Verses 13,

16, 19 set forth the principle of yielding to our members: eyes, ears, mind, hands, feet, and so forth to Christ through the indwelling of the Holy Spirit. Yielding is the definite, voluntary transference of the undivided possession, control and use of the whole being—spirit, soul, and body—from self to Christ, to Whom it rightfully belongs by creation and by purchase (I Cor. 6:19–20). When we yield all to Christ, the law of the Spirit of life frees us from the law of sin and death. Then, when that lady walks by, you see another soul for whom Christ died. This will always happen because there is no lust in the Holy Spirit. The law of the Spirit of life sets aside the law of sin, just as the Law of Aerodynamics sets aside the Law of Gravity. The Law of Gravity is not repealed; rather it is overcome but still ready to go into action. The same thing is true of the law of sin and death.

How the law of sin is continually overcome by the law of the Spirit is set forth in verse 4: *"That the righteousness of the law might be fulfilled in us, who walk not after the flesh, but after the Spirit."*

It is a daily, moment-by-moment experience as we yield to the control of the Holy Spirit. The word *"after"* is from a Greek word which means "according to, under the control of." This is clearly spelled out in the following Scriptures:

This I say then, Walk in the Spirit, and ye shall not fulfil the lust of the flesh. Gal. 5:16

If we live in the Spirit, let us also walk in the Spirit. Gal. 5:25

As ye have therefore received Christ Jesus the Lord, so walk ye in him. Col. 2:6

For we walk by faith, not by sight. II Cor. 5:7

But we had the sentence of death in ourselves, that we should not trust in ourselves, but in God which raiseth the dead. II Cor. 1:9

We cannot trust in ourselves because: *"I know that in me, (that is in my flesh), dwelleth no good thing."* (Rom. 7:18)

Let's make it really practical. You are saved, you have received the Holy Spirit, and you should start coming under the law of the Spirit, resulting in right living. However, we do not. Why? We neglect the food that is needed for spiritual growth.

As newborn babes, desire the sincere milk of the word, that ye may grow thereby. I Pet. 2:2

But grow in grace, and in the knowledge of our Lord and Saviour Jesus Christ. To Him be glory both now and for ever. Amen. II Pet. 3:18

Wherewithal shall a young man cleanse his way? By taking heed thereto according to thy word. Thy word have I hid in mine heart, that I might not sin against thee. Ps. 119:9, 11

And these words, which I command thee this day, shall be in thine heart: And thou shalt teach them diligently unto thy children, and shalt talk of them when thou sittest in thine house, and when thou walkest by the way, and when thou liest down, and when thou risest up. And thou shalt bind them for a sign upon thine hand, and they shall be as frontlets between thine eyes. And thou shalt write them upon the posts of thy house, and on thy gates. Deut. 6:6–9

As the new life is fed on the Word of God, it grows. Then, when temptation comes, that new life overcomes the law of sin and death, and you have victory! This will **always** happen.

For which cause we faint not; but though our outward man perish, yet the inward man is renewed day by day. II Cor. 4:16

But we all, with open face beholding as in a glass the glory of the Lord, are changed into the same image from glory to glory, even as by the Spirit of the Lord. II Cor. 3:18

All of this is accomplished not by self-effort—that is death—but by the Holy Spirit of God. That is **life!**

Chapter 11
Two Ways to Live Part I

In the opening paragraph of his classic book, *The Normal Christian Life*, Watchman Nee writes, "The normal Christian life…is something very different from the life of the average Christian." He goes on to write, "Indeed a consideration of the written Word of God…should lead us to ask whether such a life has ever in fact been lived upon the earth save only by the Son of God Himself."

What is the normal Christian life? It is not an improved method of living, but rather a new life.   It is not an imitation of Christ's earthly life. It is not an imagination of what Christ would do in certain situations.

It is the Holy Spirit living out the life of the Lord Jesus Christ through our humanity as we yield to Him. Romans 8:4 calls that "walking after the Spirit."

In Romans chapters 5–7, we see Christ's work on our behalf and our position in Him.

Knowing this, that our old man is crucified with him, that the body of sin might be destroyed, that henceforth we should not serve sin. Likewise reckon ye also yourselves to be dead indeed unto sin, but alive unto God through Jesus Christ our Lord. Neither yield ye your members as instruments of

unrighteousness unto sin: but yield yourselves unto God,
as those that are alive from the dead, and your members as
instruments of righteousness unto God. Rom. 6:6, 11, 13

In the first 17 verses of Romans 8, the Holy Spirit is
mentioned thirteen times. The flesh is mentioned twelve
times. We want to look at both of them to help us
understand the normal Christian life. We will look first at
what the passage teaches about living after or by the flesh.
In the next chapter, we will examine living after the Spirit.

To walk after the flesh is to live in such a way that we
derive our motivation, strength, desires, and devotion
from the Adamic or old nature, which means I have
Adam's complete provision for sinning. Notice the first
part of verse 5: *"For they that are after the flesh do mind the
things of the flesh;"* that is, those that yield themselves to
the control of the old man will act, think, and behave
according to the old man or the nature of the flesh.

The flesh will express itself in our lives in two ways:

1. Overt Acts—These are works we have no trouble
identifying. They are all fleshly.

Now the works of the flesh are manifest, which are these;
adultery, fornication, uncleanness, lasciviousness, idolatry,
witchcraft, hatred, variance, emulations, wrath, strife, seditions,
heresies, Envyings, murders, drunkenness, revellings, and such
like: of the which I tell you before, as I have also told you in
time past, that they which do such things shall not inherit the
kingdom of God. Gal. 5:19–21

For men shall be lovers of their own selves, covetous, boasters, proud, blasphemers, disobedient to parents, unthankful, unholy, Without natural affection, trucebreakers, false accusers, incontinent, fierce, despisers of those that are good, Traitors, heady, high-minded, lovers of pleasures more than lovers of God. II Tim. 3:2–4

2. Covert Acts—These have a *"form of godliness, but denying the power thereof"* (II Tim. 3:5), that is, performing religious actions of a spiritual nature in the power of the flesh. These can be praying (Matt. 6:5) to be seen of men; giving (Matt. 6:2) to have the acclaim of men; preaching or teaching (I Cor. 2:1–5); witnessing; and probably most dangerous, knowing the identification truths but not really experiencing or practicing them in our daily lives.

How does a Christian get in the position of minding the things of the flesh? Verse 6a tells us: *"For to be carnally (fleshly) minded is death."* In other words, Adam or the old nature does your thinking for you. The following quiz will give you a clue as to who is in control of your thinking.

True or False?

1. It is the job of the government to provide health care for all.

2. We can't do much about wickedness because God said it would get worse in the end times.

3. A woman is pregnant for the fifth time; her husband has a sexual disease; she has T.B. The first child was born blind, the second one died at childbirth, the third one was born deaf, and the fourth one has T.B. Should

she have an abortion? The flesh says, "Yes," and you just killed Beethoven.

4. The grocery store clerk gives you ten cents too much in change. Should you pocket it?

If you answered "true" to any of the above situations, that is Adam doing your thinking for you. The result of that is death—the death of your testimony, grieving the Holy Spirit, loss of God's power, and a troubled conscience. It is also setting in motion a sequence of sin.

But every man is tempted, when he is drawn away of his own lust, and enticed. Then when lust hath conceived, it bringeth forth sin: and sin, when it is finished, bringeth forth death.
James 1:14–15

Romans 8:7 gives us the reason for this: *"Because the carnal mind is enmity* (it is marshaled under a hostile banner) *against God* (it is militantly opposed to God): *for it is not subject to the law of God, neither indeed can be."*

That is why there is conflict in our lives, just as Paul recorded in Romans 7. That is why a Christian can know intellectually all the facts of identification with Christ in His death, burial and resurrection, can know the way of victory over sin, and yet be defeated. The defeated Christian is one who knows all these facts and attempts to practice them in the flesh. The result is always the same— defeat! That is the law of the flesh, and verse 8 says that they that are in the flesh **cannot** please God!

"O wretched man that I am! who shall deliver me from the body of this death? I thank God through Jesus Christ our Lord."

Chapter 12
Two Ways to Live Part II

In the previous chapter, we looked at living after, or under, the control of the flesh. The other side of that is to live after the Spirit, or to be spiritually minded. The result of being spiritually minded is life and peace (verse 6). It is obvious that this is the opposite of verses 7 and 8.

We then must ask, "What does it mean to be spiritually minded?" It does not mean to spend all our time reading or memorizing Scripture, nor preaching on street corners. It does not mean saying "hallelujah" or "amen" with every other breath, nor does it mean spiritual superiority over other believers. It means allowing the mind of Christ to control our thoughts, our wills, and our actions. In I Corinthians 2:16, we are told that we have the mind of Christ, and in Philippians 2:5, that we are to let the mind of Christ be in us. When we received Jesus as Savior, we received His mind, and we are commanded to let His mind be the controlling influence in our lives.

How does this work out in the nitty-gritty of our daily lives?

1. Seek the mind of the Lord through His Word for all our actions.

Then they told David, saying, Behold, the Philistines fight against Keilah, and they rob the threshing floors. Therefore David enquired of the LORD, saying, Shall I go and smite these Philistines? And the LORD said unto David, Go, and smite the Philistines, and save Keilah. I Sam. 23:1–2

And David enquired at the LORD, saying, Shall I pursue after this troop? Shall I overtake them? And he answered him, Pursue: for thou shalt surely overtake them, and without fail recover all. I Sam. 30:8

In these verses, David sought the mind of the Lord before he made any moves. Moses could say with assurance in Numbers 16:28: *"...Hereby ye shall know that the LORD hath sent me to do all these works; for I have not done them of mine own mind."*

2. Admit that we cannot do what the Lord wants us to do.

For my thoughts are not your thoughts, neither are your ways my ways, saith the LORD. For as the heavens are higher than the earth, so are my ways higher than your ways, and my thoughts than your thoughts. Is. 55:8–9

It is allowing the Holy Spirit to do our thinking for us in ALL the daily activities of life. Since God knows in advance the outcome of actions or decisions, we need to look to Him. So—Lord, should I take this job, move to this town, buy this car, etc? Since to be spiritually minded is life and peace, we need to ask how this can be ours.

Verse 9a makes it clear that this is written to believers: "But ye are not in the flesh, but in the Spirit, if so be since the Spirit of God dwell in you."

Know ye not that ye are the temple of God, and that the Spirit of God dwelleth in you? I Cor. 3:16

What? Know ye not that your body is the temple of the Holy Ghost which is in you, which ye have of God, and ye are not your own? For ye are bought with a price: therefore, glorify God in your body, and in your spirit, which are God's. I Cor. 6:19–20

Do you have the Holy Spirit? Was there a time when you saw yourself as a sinner?

But God commendeth his love toward us, in that, while we were yet sinners, Christ died for us. Rom. 5:8

As it is written, There is none righteous, no not one: Rom. 3:10

For all have sinned, and come short of the glory of God. Rom. 3:23

For the wages of sin is death; but the gift of God is eternal life through Jesus Christ our Lord. Rom. 6:23

All we like sheep have gone astray; we have turned every one to his own way; and the LORD hath laid on him the iniquity of us all. Is. 53:6

Christ took your death to give you His life. If you have never trusted Him, do so now.

But as many as received him, to them gave he power to become the sons of God, even to them that believe on his name. Jn. 1:12

For whosoever shall call upon the name of the Lord shall be saved. Rom. 10:13

Behold, I stand at the door, and knock: if any man hear my voice, and open the door, I will come in to him, and will sup with him, and he with me. Rev. 3:20

If verse 9a is true of you, that is, you have trusted Christ as Savior, but you find yourself thinking in terms of the world and the flesh, how do you change that?

I beseech you therefore, brethren, by the mercies of God, that ye present your bodies a living sacrifice, holy, acceptable unto God, which is your reasonable service. And be not conformed to this world: but be ye transformed by the renewing of your mind, that ye may prove what is that good, and acceptable, and perfect, will of God. Rom. 12:1–2

Thou will keep him in perfect peace whose mind is stayed on thee: because he trusteth in thee. Trust ye in the LORD for ever: for in the LORD JEHOVAH is everlasting strength. Is. 26:3–4

Finally, brethren, whatsoever things are true, whatsoever things are honest, whatsoever things are just, whatsoever things are pure, whatsoever things are lovely, whatsoever things are of good report; if there be any virtue, and if there be any praise, think on these things. Phil. 4:8

Confess the wrong thinking as sin and begin to fill your mind with God's Word.

Blessed is the man that walketh not in the counsel of the ungodly, nor standeth in the way of sinners, not sitteth in the

seat of the scornful. But his delight is in the law of the LORD;
and in his law doth he meditate day and night. Ps. 1:1–2

Wherewithal shall a young man cleanse his way? By taking
heed thereto according to thy word. Thy word have I hid in
mine heart that I might not sin against thee. Order my steps
in thy word: and let not any iniquity have dominion over me.
Ps. 119:9, 11, 133

3. Submit ourselves totally to the control of the Holy Spirit.

As long as we continue to think we can live a life pleasing
to the Lord in our strength or ability, we will be defeated.
As we realize that we cannot, but HE can, and we yield to
His control, we will have victory.

Neither yield ye your members as instruments of
unrighteousness unto sin: but yield yourselves unto God,
as those that are alive from the dead, and your members as
instruments of righteousness unto God. Know ye not, that to
whom ye yield yourselves as servants to obey, his servants ye are
to whom ye obey; whether of sin unto death, or of obedience unto
righteousness? But God be thanked, that ye were the servants
of sin, but ye have obeyed from the heart that form of doctrine
which was delivered you. Being then made free from sin, ye
became the servants of righteousness. Rom. 6:13, 16–18

This is the best way to live! What is the means that makes
this true in our lives? Allow the indwelling Spirit to apply
the Word of God to every thought, word, and action. As
you yield moment-by-moment to the Holy Spirit's control,

He applies the Word of God to your decisions and actions, and you have life and peace.